Bull Riding

Josepha Sherman

Heinemann Library
Chicago, Illinois

The Most Dangerous Event

Nobody goes home from a rodeo before the bull riding event!

It has been a long day at the rodeo. Calves have been roped and bucking **broncs** have been ridden. The air is dusty and full of the smells of horses and **cattle**. In the grandstands, children are getting restless and adults are stretching.

But nobody in the audience wants to leave. They know that the wildest and most dangerous rodeo event is still to come. That event is the bull riding competition.

Why is bull riding so dangerous? Aren't bulls just male cattle, the way cows are female cattle? Yes, but a bull is far from being a friendly dairy animal. A 2,000-pound (907 kilogram) bull hates being ridden. Once the bull throws a cowboy, he may try to use his horns to **gore** the fallen man, or he may try to trample the unlucky rider under sharp hooves. This is why bull riding is rodeo's greatest challenge.

An angry bull is a dangerous ride!

The Riders: Beginners

How does someone become a bull rider? One way is to start with children's rodeo events for boys five years old or younger. A boy that young isn't expected to ride a bull, but he is allowed to try staying on the back of a sheep. A sheep doesn't like being ridden, but it isn't really dangerous. And there isn't far to fall when a rider gets thrown.

Once a boy is more than six years old, he can graduate to riding calves. Calves don't want to be ridden, either, and they will buck. But calves are too young and too small to do more than dump a rider into the dirt.

A boy tries his hand at sheep riding.

A calf doesn't have horns like a steer or bull.

Older boys, up to about fourteen years of age, can try riding **steers.** A steer is the size of a cow but is far gentler than a bull. However, a steer can still put up quite a show of bucking.

By the time a boy is in his midteens, he's eligible to ride bulls in the junior divisions. Once he's proved himself ready by winning or placing in enough events, he can move on to become a true bull rider. There are no rules that keep girls out of bull riding, but most bull riders are men.

The Riders: Schooling

A rider must learn to lean forward to avoid being bucked off by the bull.

Another way to learn to become a bull rider is by going to school. Bull riding schools teach the rules and skills of the sport. One advantage of attending a bull riding school is that the instructor is a rodeo professional. Another advantage of the school is the opportunity to practice on something other than live and dangerous bulls.

Practice can be done on a **bull-riding machine**. This type of machine looks like a robotic bull. The **barrel**, or body, is there, complete with a **bull rope** around the machine's middle or a handle sticking from its back. A motor makes the machine buck, pitch, and spin like a live bull. And it can be very difficult to ride.

The machine is a good way for a rider to develop his style without worrying about getting trampled. But bull riders also need practice sessions on live animals. These are held in practice pens. Practice keeps the bull rider's skills sharp without putting him in too much danger.

A cowboy practices on a mechanical bull.

The Riders: Professionals

A rodeo clown rushes to help a fallen cowboy.

Bulls hate being ridden. Many bulls hate being ridden so much that they become known as "head hunters." A head hunter bull deliberately tries to hurt or even kill cowboys. Most professional bull riders have broken bones or lost teeth during competitions. One rider, World Champion Lane Frost, was killed following a ride in 1989 when he was **gored** by the bull.

Why do cowboys take part in such a dangerous sport? Cowboys don't choose bull riding for the prize money. Prizes for riding a bull are the same as for any safer, major rodeo event. And a successful bull rider has as much chance of winning a world championship as any good rodeo cowboy. So why do they do it? Some cowboys say they enjoy the challenge and triumph that comes with a successful ride. Other say it's the battle of nerves between a rider and a bull that keeps them coming back.

Bull riding is not an easy way to make a living! The average bull rider enters between thirty and eighty rodeos a year. Eighty rodeos means 80 rides on a 2,000-pound (907 kilogram) animal that wants to get the cowboy off his back and maybe even kill him. So the question still stands. Why do cowboys take part in such a dangerous sport?

A good ride could bring this cowboy thousands of dollars.

The Rules

The rules of bull riding sound very simple. A bull is driven into a closed **chute** that's only big enough for him. A cowboy slides gingerly onto his back. The chute gate flings open, and the bull leaps out into the rodeo arena. Instantly it begins to buck and spin about. All the cowboy has to do is stay on the bull's back for eight seconds.

But eight seconds can be a very long time when the bull doesn't want the cowboy on his back. It seems even longer when the bull can buck and twist like a humongous cat with a terrible temper.

It's dangerous just being in the pen on an angry bull's back.

bull rope

All there is for the cowboy to hang onto is the **bull rope**. This is a narrow rope of braided leather tied about the bull's middle, just behind the shoulders. The cowboy is only allowed to hold onto that rope with one hand. If the cowboy's free hand touches the bull or the rope for even a second, the cowboy is disqualified. There is a weighted cowbell hanging from the bottom of the bull rope. This is a bell that serves as a weight to help the rope slide off the bull once the cowboy lets go.

Judging The Ride

This cowboy is in for a wild ride!

Although an eight-second timer is used, bull riding is not considered a timed event. It is called a scored event.

Two judges make sure that the rules are followed. They also rate each rider. The judges decide who is the winner.

How do judges score a ride? First, of course, the rider must stay on the bull until a buzzer lets everyone know that eight seconds are up.

A cowboy must also show good style while he is on the bull's back. Judges are looking for good body position, which means that the cowboy looks as though he is still in control of the ride. Judges are also looking for style, but it's not necessary for a bull rider to spur the bull, as it is in the **bronc** riding events. Hanging on and staying right side up are the bull riding cowboy's top priority.

But the rider's style makes up only half the score. The other half is earned by the bull. Not every bull is a good performer, and not every bull wants to give his best in every rodeo. A really good bucking bull who is difficult to ride and flashy to watch can make the winning difference for a cowboy.

Spurring isn't required, but it can add points to a bull rider's score.

17

Getting Off!

Once a man has stayed on a bull for eight seconds, he's faced with a new problem. How does he get off? In **bronc** riding events, a cowboy sometimes just jumps off, because he knows that the bronc won't try to attack him. A bronc rider can also wait for a **pickup man**—the mounted cowboy who helps a bronc rider off the horse.

But pickup men can't be used in bull riding events, because the bull would attack the horse. The cowboy is faced with two choices. He can jump off or he can fall off. Either way, the cowboy will find himself confronted by a very angry bull.

Once a cowboy finishes his eight second ride, he still has the problem of getting away.

A rodeo clown has to be fast and fit.

There is still another problem for the cowboy who is trying to get off of a bull. The **bull rope** that he's been clutching can sometimes wrap about his arm or hand. When he tries to jump off, he gets hung up, or caught on the rope, and finds himself hanging from the bull. His own body weight keeps the rope from unfastening from about the bull.

At this point, one of the most valuable people in bull riding goes to work. This man has been called the cowboy's best friend. This life saver is the **rodeo clown.**

The Rodeo Clowns

The **rodeo clown** performs between rodeo events. He wears funny makeup, does humorous stunts, entertains the audience, and plays pranks on the announcer, just like a circus clown. But a rodeo clown's most important job is to distract the bull and protect the cowboy.

The rodeo clown usually is a **barrelman**, too. He hides in a rubber **barrel**, popping in and out to attract or duck the bull. Of course, the reason he's in the barrel is because he's not about to challenge the bull.

Another clown who challenges the bull is the bullfighting clown, or bullfighter. He is a trained athlete and not a **comedian.** This is the clown that helps the fallen cowboy after a bull ride. The bullfighting clown might also stage a demonstration with other bullfighters against the bulls to show off the bravery, skill, and agility of the bullfighting clown.

A clown in a barrel confuses a bull.

No matter what a clown's specialty, comedy or bullfighting, a bull rider can depend on him. As the cowboy makes his break to the safety of the grandstand, the clown waves at the bull or teases him. He does everything possible to keep the bull's attention away from the cowboy.

This is very dangerous for the clown, of course. A bull is fast and can turn so quickly that he's unpredictable. An angry bull wants to hurt or kill anyone he can reach. Sometimes clowns do get hurt, but by risking their lives, they save others.

Bulls used for rodeo bullfighting are bred to be smaller and faster than the bulls used for bull riding.

A Rider and His Gear

Cowboys come in all shapes and sizes!

There are no set rules about the size or weight of a good bull rider. Some cowboys are tall, while others may be short. The weight of riders can vary a lot from one cowboy to another, too. But most bull riders are on the shorter side, rather than the taller. And most of them are very solidly built. There really aren't any skinny or overweight bull riders, because all bull riders have to be in good physical condition.

A good bull rider needs good equipment, too. He may spend more than $300 a year on his **bull rope** and his spurs. A wise rider also owns a good **protective vest** called a Flak Jacket. That vest can save his life if the bull tries to **gore** or trample him.

How a cowboy feels about bull riding is as important as how strong he may be or whether he has the proper equipment. If a cowboy doesn't believe he can win, then bull riding may not be his event.

Flak Jacket

Chaps   Gloves

Rodeo Stars: Men and Bulls

Larry Mahan

Larry Mahan holds six rodeo world championships and a place of honor in the ProRodeo Hall of Fame. Mahan is now retired from competition, but he remains one of the most successful bull riders ever. Mahan can sometimes be seen as a television announcer for rodeo events.

Tuff Hedeman

This three-time rodeo world champion earned his title with bull riding. Tuff Hedeman was a partner of Lane Frost, the bull rider who was killed in 1989. In honor of Frost, Tuff Hedeman rode a bull that year an extra eight seconds. The only bull to really get the better of him was the champion bull Bodacious.

Tuff Hedeman shows the bull who's boss in 1991.

Bodacious

When bull riders talk about this champion bucking bull, their voices take on a note of respect. Bodacious, a strongly muscled animal with a golden hide, was one of the most dangerous bulls. Almost no one could ride him for even a few seconds. Yet for all his fierceness, Bodacious definitely had star quality. He is now retired, and great things are expected of his offspring.

You don't have to be a bull rider to become a legend. Some bulls, like Bodacious, have become famous on their own!

Bull Riding beyond the Rodeo

The world of bull riding is a big one. Bull riding takes place beyond the rodeo arena and even beyond North America. There is a bull riding association in Okinawa that was started by U.S. soldiers stationed there. Bull riding, as well as other rodeo events, can also be found in Australia, New Zealand, and Japan, as well as in Europe.

In any part of the world, bull riding is a dangerous sport.

No one is sure if this ancient painting shows a sport or a religious ritual.

Bull riding has been around for a very long time. On the walls of the ancient city of Knossos, on the Greek island of Crete, there are three-thousand-year-old paintings that show people doing a form of bull riding—leaping on and off the bull's back and **vaulting** over his horns. Maybe there always have been people wanting to test their skill and courage against a creature as dangerous as a bull.

Associations

American Junior
    Bull Riders Association
P.O. Box 905
Azle, Tex. 7698-0905
(817) 444-2282
Fax: (817) 270-2297

Bull Riders of America
12499 East Remie Road
Centralia, Mo. 65240
(573) 696-7253

International Professional
    Rodeo Association
P.O. Box 83377
Oklahoma City, Okla. 73148
(800) 458-4772

National Federation of
    Professional Bull Riders
222 Highway F
Mansfield, Mo. 56704

Bull Riding Winners

Prize Money

Bull riding isn't an easy way to make a living, but a good rider can make good money. Through 1998, Ty Murray had earned over a million dollars at the rodeo. He also holds the record for the most money won in a single year. In 1993 his prize total was $297,896.

Most Money Won at Regular-Season Rodeo

$31,010 by Ty Murray at Houston Livestock Show and Rodeo, 1994

Most Money Won at a Single Rodeo

$124,821 by Ty Murray, 1993 National Finals Rodeo

Most Bull Riding Titles Held

8   Don Gay

Most Consecutive Bull Riding Titles Held

6   Jim Shoulders, 1954–1959

Recent Bull Riding Champions

1990	Dustin Young	1995	Ken Stillman
1991	Casey Allred	1996	Tony Mendes
1992	Jessie Allred	1997	J.C. Sanders
1993	Greg Richins	1998	Cody Hancock
1994	J.C. Sanders		

Glossary

barrel   large, cylindrical container; also, the midsection of a bull or horse

barrelman   rodeo clown who hides in a rubber barrel and pops in and out of it to attract the bull

Brahma   breed of cattle that originated in India

bronc   bucking horse in a rodeo, also called a bronco

bull-riding machine   machine that imitates the movements of a bucking bull and that bull riders use to practice their skills

bull rope   rope of braided leather tied around the bull's middle, an end of which the rider holds onto with one hand

cattle   bulls, cows, steers, and calves

chaps   leather coverings worn over pants to protect a cowboy's legs

chute   narrow pen that holds an animal, so that the rider can get on its back

comedian   performer who does funny things, which are called comedy

gore   to wound with a horn

Hereford   breed of cattle raised for their milk

pickup man   rider who helps bronc riders off the horse when their ride is done, and who leads the horse from the arena

protective vest   heavily padded, sleeveless jacket that protects a rider's chest

purebred animal whose ancestors all belong to one breed

steer young adult male cattle that cannot reproduce

rodeo clown athletic performer who protects contestants in dangerous situations by distracting the animals, and who sometimes entertains the rodeo audience with clown antics

vaulting using the hands to help jump over something

More Books to Read

Acton, Avis. *Behind the Chutes at Cheyenne Frontier Days: Your Pocket Guide to Rodeo.* Cheyenne, Wyo.: A B C Publishing, 1991.

Bellville, Cheryl. *Rodeo.* Minneapolis: Lerner Publishing Group, 1985.

Greenberg, Keith. *Rodeo Clown: Laughs & Danger in the Ring.* Woodbridge, Conn.: Blackbirch Press, 1995.

Index